This coloring book bel

HAPPY EASTER!

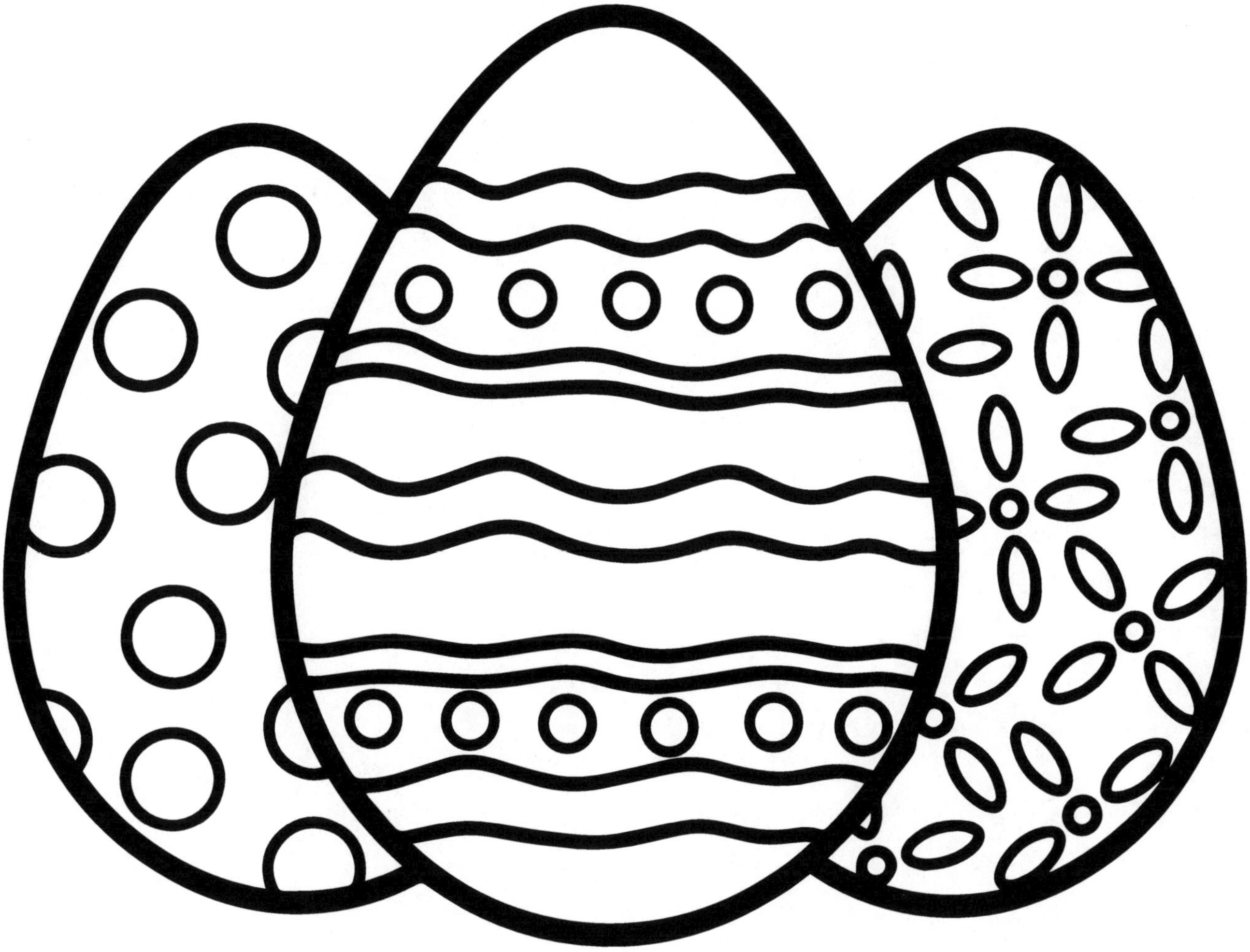

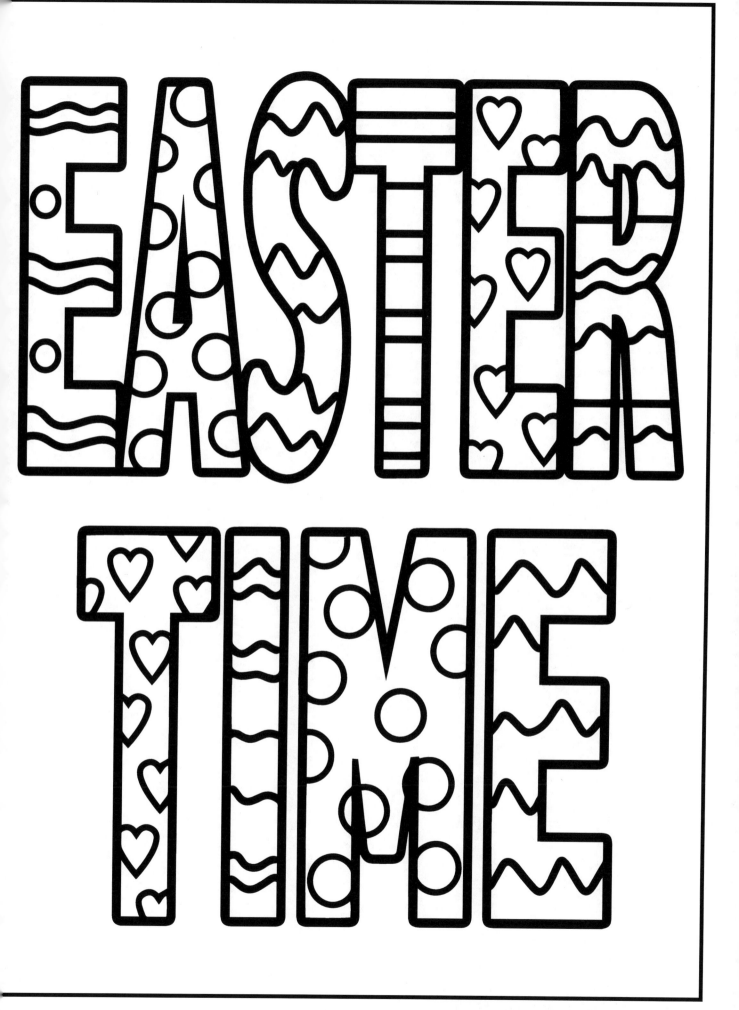

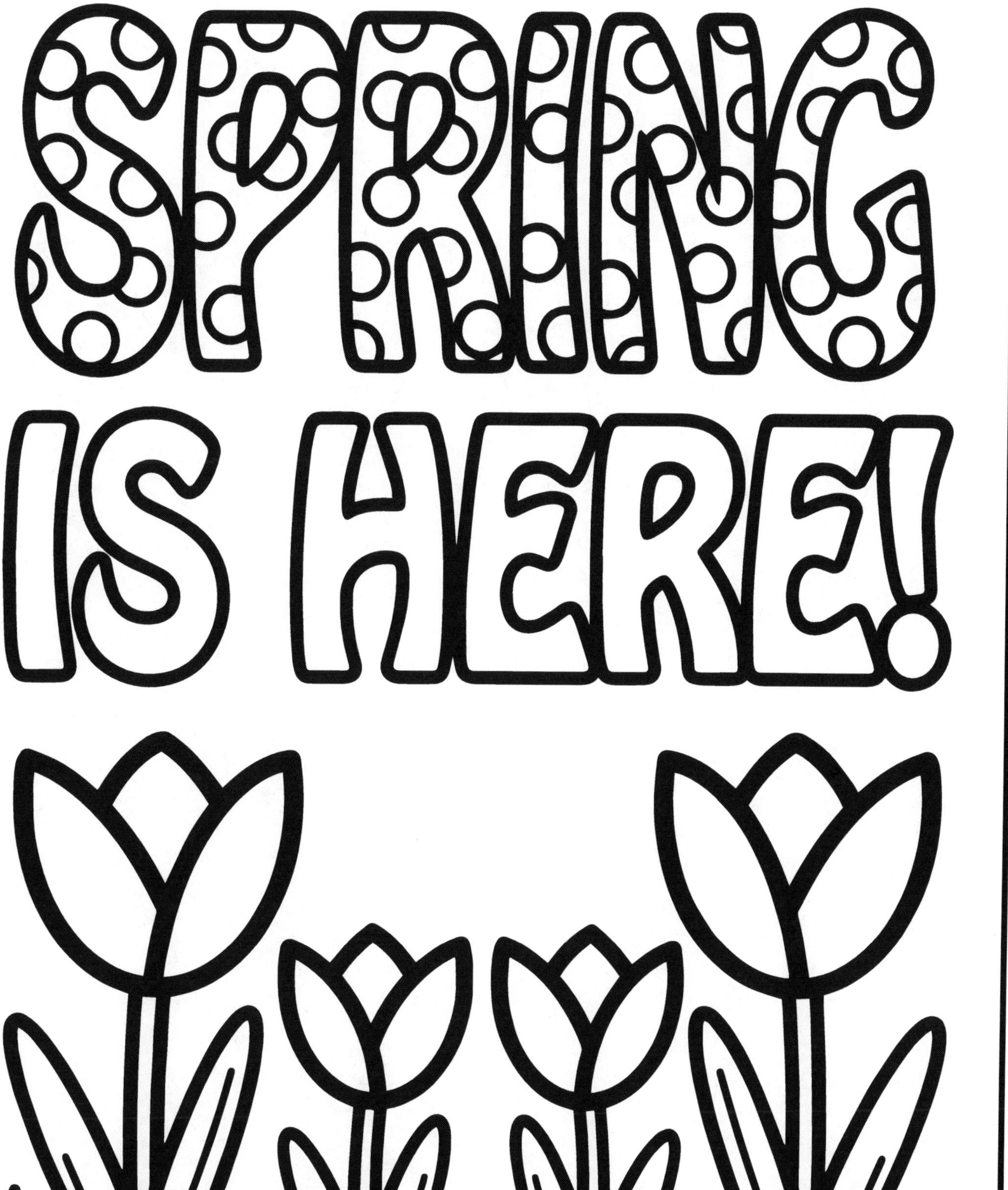
SPRING
IS HERE!

SPRING TIME!

Made in the USA
Columbia, SC
28 March 2023

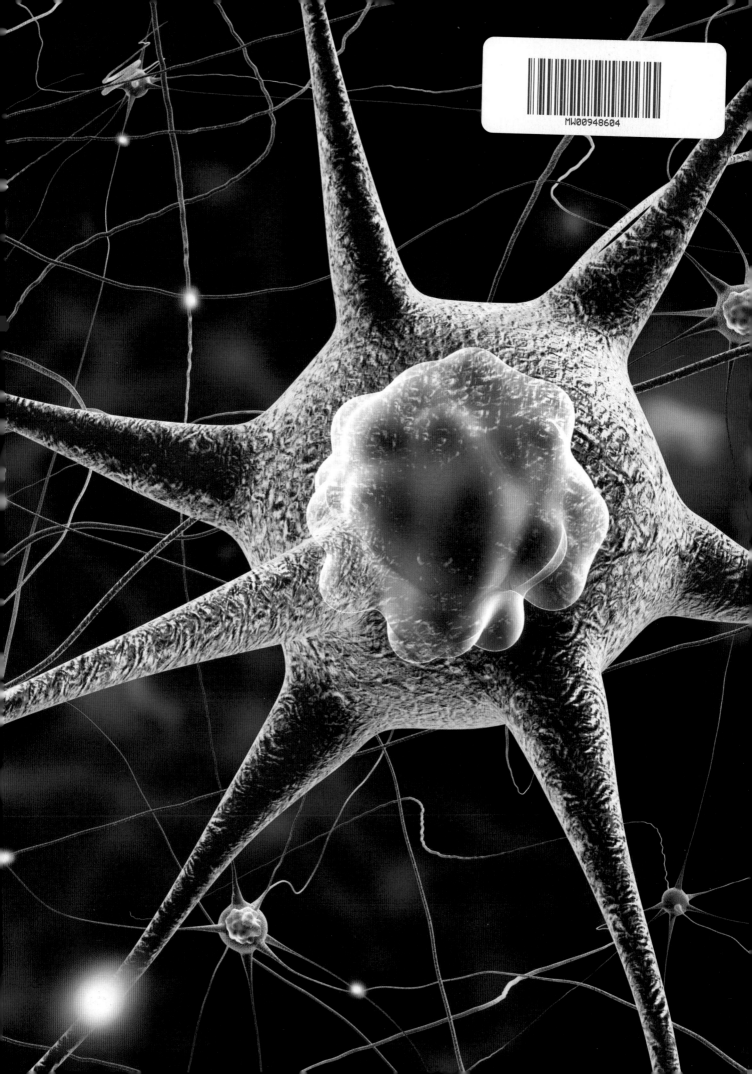

DISCOVER
BIOLOGY

Predominant artwork & imagery source:
Shutterstock.com

Copyright: North Parade Publishing Ltd.

4 North Parade,

Bath,

BA1 1LF, UK

First Published: 2018

Printed in China.

Contents

INTRODUCTION TO CELLS   6

ANIMAL AND PLANT CELLS   8

CELL DIVISION   10

CELL TRANSPORT   12

CELL AND TISSUE ORGANIZATION   13

CHROMOSOMES AND GENES   14

GENETIC ENGINEERING   16

CLONING   18

MICROSCOPY   20

GROWING MICROBES IN THE LAB   22

DISEASES   24

IMMUNITY   26

CLASSIFICATION OF ORGANISMS   28

BIOENERGETICS: PHOTOSYNTHESIS   30

BIOENERGETICS: RESPIRATION, METABOLISM AND HOMEOSTASIS   32

HUMAN SYSTEMS   34

GENETICS   38

EVOLUTION   40

ECOSYSTEMS   42

INTERACTION WITH ENVIRONMENT   44

Introduction to Cells

All living things are made of cells. A cell is the most basic structural and functional unit of a living being. Some organisms (for example, bacteria) are single cells. Others, like plants and animals, are made up of billions of cells.

◀ *Our skin is made of billions of skin cells that act as a protective barrier and a sensory organ*

▲ *A bacterium is a single-celled organism that can co-exist with other bacteria in chains or clumps*

Discovery of Cells

Cells were first discovered by Robert Hooke in 1665. He used a crude microscope he invented to observe a thin slice of cork. He saw a lot of tiny pore-like structures. He coined the term 'cell' as they resembled the small rooms where the monks lived called 'cella' in Latin. Interest in the study of cells and the beginning of a separate field called 'cell biology' began. The cell theory was proposed by Theodor Schwann and Matthias Schleiden. It states that all living organisms are made up of cells, the basic units, which can arise only from the division of other cells.

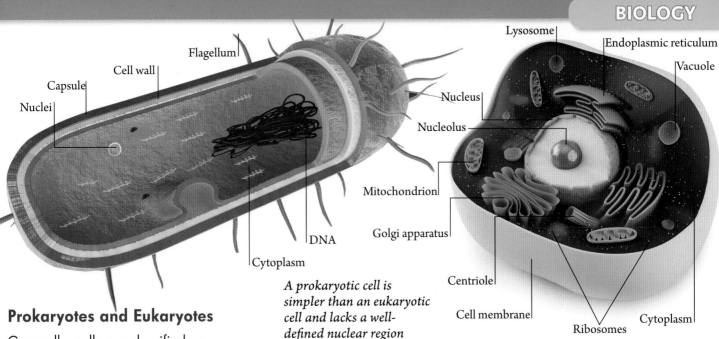

A prokaryotic cell is simpler than an eukaryotic cell and lacks a well-defined nuclear region

Prokaryotes and Eukaryotes

Generally, cells are classified as prokaryotes or eukaryotes.

Prokaryotes: (Pro – primitive, karyote – nucleus): As the name suggests, prokaryotes have primitive nuclear material. There is no well-defined nucleus and the genetic material (DNA) is not arranged in the form of chromosomes. Instead, it is found as a single, compact loop that contains all the information to code for proteins needed for the cell to survive and reproduce. Prokaryotes were the only life forms on Earth for millions of years until more complex eukaryotes evolved.

Eukaryotes: (Eu – True, karyote – nucleus): The defining feature of a eukaryotic cell is the presence of a well-defined region where the genetic material is concentrated. This region is called the nucleus. The nucleus is covered by a nuclear membrane.

Prokaryotes

1. Contain genetic material as a single circular loop

2. Do not have a well-defined nucleus or specialized site for DNA

3. The genome is very compact and contains only regions that code for proteins

4. No well-defined membrane-bound organelles present

5. Possess complex cell walls that vary from one organism to another

6. Usually unicellular

Eukaryotes

1. Contain genetic material as linear chromosomes

2. Have a well-defined nucleus with nuclear envelope and nucleolus

3. The genome has large chunks of repetitive DNA that does not code for any proteins

4. Well-defined membrane-bound organelles present

5. Cell walls are absent except in plants and algae

6. Usually multicellular

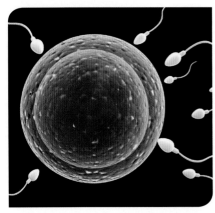

▲ *The egg cell (ovum) is among the largest cells in the human body and can measure up to 0.1mm*

Size of Cells

Individual cells are microscopic, this means they can only be viewed under the magnification of a microscope. The size of cells varies greatly. An amoeba is about 0.1 millimetre in size (one tenth of a millimetre) and can be viewed with the naked eye under the right conditions. Similarly, a human egg cell is comparatively large in size. On the other hand, red blood cells are among the smallest cells in the human body.

Fact File

The average size of prokaryotes is 1 – 10 micrometres. (One micrometre is one thousandth of a millimetre). Eukaryotic cells range in size from 10 – 100 micrometres.

Animal and Plant Cells

Animal cells possess a well-defined plasma membrane as well as membrane bound organelles. Plant cells have a prominent cell wall that is absent in animal cells. While plant cells can produce their own food from sunlight, animal cells are capable of locomotion, enabled by the lack of cell walls.

Organelles are components of animal cells that are involved in specific functions. They include:

Plasma membrane: A protective membrane that protects the cell and contains all the organelles.

Nucleus: It is the most important part of the cell and contains all the DNA (genetic information) needed for the growth, activities and reproduction of the cell.

Mitochondria: Called the 'powerhouse of the cell', they convert oxygen and nutrients into energy.

Endoplasmic reticulum (ER): A network of sacs that manufactures, processes, and transports chemical compounds.

Golgi apparatus: It helps in distributing the chemical compounds produced in ER outside the cell.

Ribosomes: Tiny organelles made up of RNA (ribonucleic acid) and proteins, which help with protein synthesis.

Lysosomes: Double membrane organelles containing enzymes that assist in digestion.

Centrioles: Made of nine bundles of microtubules, they assist in cell division.

Flagella/Cilia: Extensions that help in locomotion.

Microfilaments, microtubules and intermediate filaments: Provide structural support to the cell.

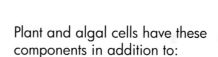

Plant and algal cells have these components in addition to:

Cell wall: A protective layer that provides support and structure to the cell.

Chloroplasts: These organelles are involved in photosynthesis, a process by which plants make their own food from sunlight.

Vacuoles: A storage organelle that contains essential chemical compounds and assists growth.

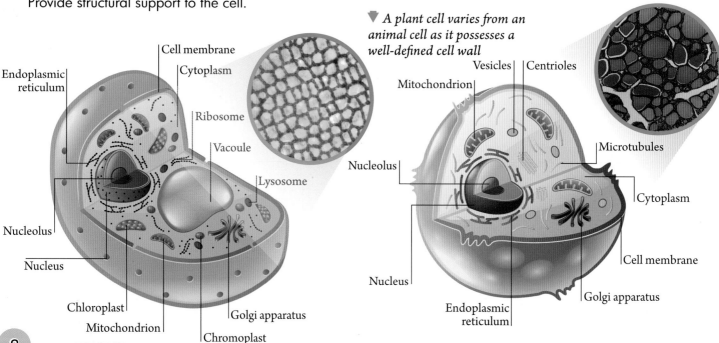

▼ *A plant cell varies from an animal cell as it possesses a well-defined cell wall*

Endoplasmic reticulum

Cell membrane

Cytoplasm

Ribosome

Vacuole

Lysosome

Nucleolus

Nucleus

Chloroplast

Mitochondrion

Golgi apparatus

Chromoplast

Vesicles

Centrioles

Mitochondrion

Nucleolus

Microtubules

Cytoplasm

Nucleus

Cell membrane

Endoplasmic reticulum

Golgi apparatus

Cell Differentiation

The process by which a young, immature cell develops into a specialized cell capable of a specific function is called cell differentiation. Any cell that is capable of this process of evolving into another cell is said to be 'totipotent'. Some cells, like the stem cells in animals and the meristematic cells in higher plants, can differentiate into different types of cells. Such cells are 'pluripotent'.

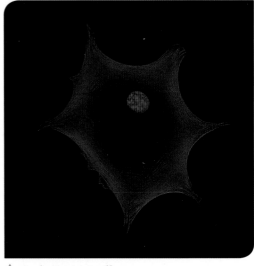

▲ *A pluripotent cell can differentiate into any type of cell*

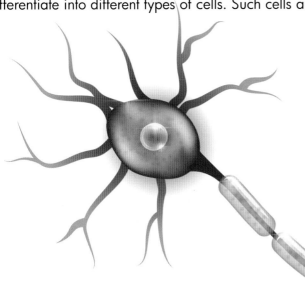

◀ *A neuron is a specialized cell that communicates through electrical signals*

Cell Specialization

In single-celled organisms, all the functions for survival and reproduction are present in the cell. Multicellular organisms are more complex. Certain cell groups are assigned a specific function and such cells are called 'specialized cells'. Depending on their purpose and function, cell groups may have different sizes, shapes and cellular makeup. The difference in structure and function of the cells happens at the genetic level – that is, certain genes are activated to make a cell specialized in its particular function.

Let us look at some examples of specialized cells:

Neuron: Also called a nerve cell, it can grow to be about a metre in length. Nerve cells transmit signals from different parts of the body to the brain.

Red blood cell: This is a button-shaped cell that contains the pigment hemoglobin. Red blood cells carry oxygen from the lungs to different parts of the body and bring carbon dioxide from the body to the lungs.

Root hair cell: It is a specialized cell that is present in the root. These cells have hair-like projections to absorb nutrients and water.

Guard cell: Present on leaves and stems, guard cells open, close and control the stomata through which plants exchange water and carbon dioxide.

Fact File

An adult human has more than 200 specialized cells in their body to perform different functions.

▶ *Cells specialize to perform specific functions*

Cell Division

The cells in our body divide all the time and make new cells. Old cells are replaced by newer cells. A single cell divides into two, and these two cells can produce four cells and so on. This process is called 'cell division'. We began life as a single cell and by the time we become adults, there are trillions of cells in our bodies.

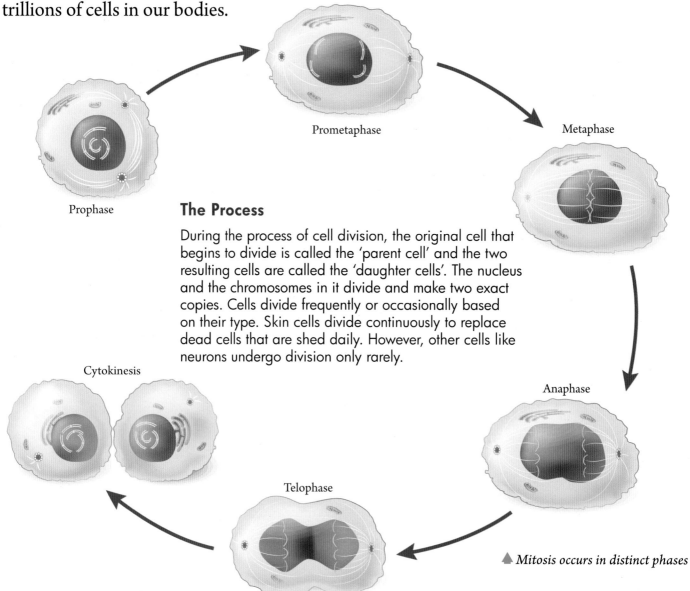

Prophase

Prometaphase

Metaphase

Cytokinesis

Anaphase

Telophase

Mitosis occurs in distinct phases

The Process

During the process of cell division, the original cell that begins to divide is called the 'parent cell' and the two resulting cells are called the 'daughter cells'. The nucleus and the chromosomes in it divide and make two exact copies. Cells divide frequently or occasionally based on their type. Skin cells divide continuously to replace dead cells that are shed daily. However, other cells like neurons undergo division only rarely.

Mitosis

The process by which non-reproductive, regular cells undergo cell division is called mitosis. When the parent cell divides into two daughter cells, the newly-formed cells have the same number of chromosomes as the parent.

Meiosis

Meiosis is the process by which a parent cell divides twice to form four daughter cells, each having only half the number of chromosomes as the parent. Meiosis is responsible for the production of sperm in males and eggs in females. Since a sperm and an egg have only half the set of chromosomes, when they fuse, the new cell will have the complete set of chromosomes from both the parent cells.

Fact File

We lose about 50 million skin cells every day, and they are replaced through skin cell division.

Cell Cycle

Cells that are actively dividing go through several stages collectively known as the cell cycle. The stages are:

Gap 1 Phase: The cell prepares for division by undergoing certain metabolic changes.

Synthesis Phase: DNA synthesis occurs and the genetic material in the nucleus undergoes replication.

Gap 2 Phase: Metabolic changes occur to produce more cytoplasm as the cell prepares for division.

Mitosis Phase: Division of the nucleus (called nucleokinesis) and the division of the entire cell (called cytokinesis) occur in this phase.

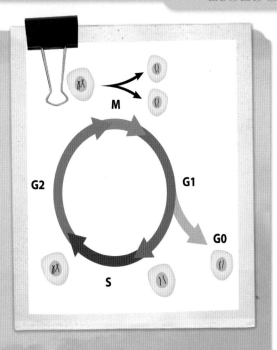

Stem Cells

Stem cells are remarkable in that they have the ability to differentiate into a range of different specialized cells such as bone, skin, blood and many others. Stem cells remain dormant for years and then can be activated to replace cells that are lost or damaged.

The two main types of stem cells are:

1. Embryonic Stem Cells: These stem cells provide all the different types of cells that a developing embryo needs as it grows into a baby. They are 'pluripotent' and capable of developing into any type of cell.

2. Adult Stem Cells: Found in the bone marrow, they can replace damaged cells in a full-grown adult. They are 'multipotent', that is they can differentiate into certain types of cells, but not all.

Scientists have identified many useful purposes for stem cells. In the laboratory, stem cells can be induced to produce entire organs such as skin and heart. They can also be used for producing blood cells in patients who have lost their blood cells due to cancer or any other disease.

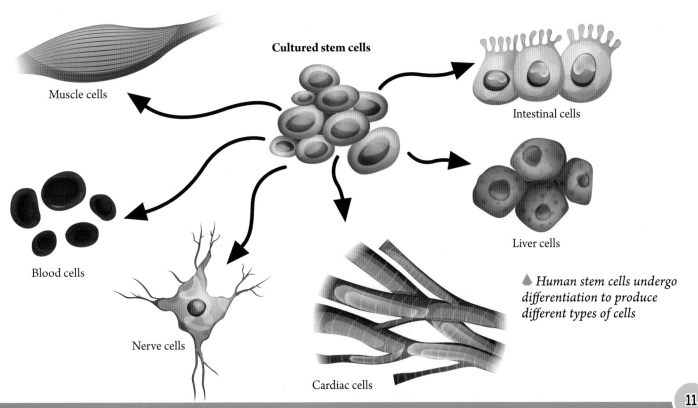

Muscle cells

Cultured stem cells

Intestinal cells

Liver cells

Blood cells

Nerve cells

Cardiac cells

▲ *Human stem cells undergo differentiation to produce different types of cells*

Cell Transport

Movement of materials and water in and out of the cell occur due to the semi-permeable nature of the membrane. This is known as cell transport. Cell transport can be active or passive: active transport requires energy, passive transport does not.

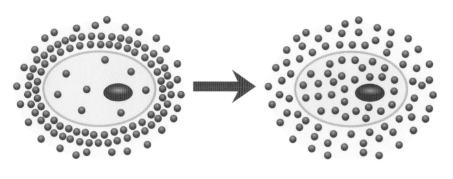

Fact File

Gap junction is a type of passive transport mechanism that enables the heart muscles to contract in a coordinated, smooth manner.

▲ *The semi-permeable membrane allows movement of molecules*

Passive Transport

1. Simple Diffusion: Diffusion is a process by which molecules move from a region of higher concentration to a region of lower concentration. The difference in concentration between the two regions is called a 'concentration gradient'. Diffusion usually continues until the concentration is uniform on both sides. Some of the factors that affect diffusion are:

1. Surface area of the membrane

2. Temperature

3. Concentration gradient

2. Facilitated Diffusion: When diffusion occurs with the help of a carrier protein, it is known as facilitated diffusion. Each carrier protein is of a specific shape and only allows specific molecules to pass through.

3. Osmosis: Osmosis is a type of diffusion that occurs in the presence of a semi-permeable membrane. Here, water travels from a less concentrated solution to a more concentrated one. Roots absorb water from the soil through osmosis.

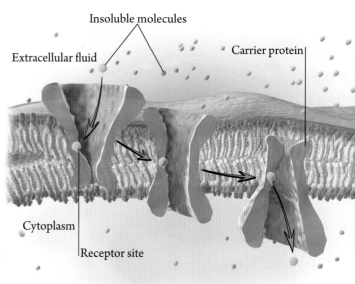

▲ *Carrier proteins are important in facilitated passive transport*

Active Transport

The movement of molecules from a region of lower concentration to a region of higher concentration is called active transport. Active transport requires energy which is usually supplied by the mitochondria in the cells in the form of ATP (Adenosine Tri Phosphate). This method is used for bringing in glucose, ions and amino acids that the cell needs.

◀ *Active transport utilizes energy in the form of ATP molecules*

Cell and Tissue Organization

In a simple one-celled organism, such as an Amoeba living in a pond, nutrients are absorbed directly from the environment and the wastes excreted out. In complex multicellular organisms, specialized systems are needed to carry out different functions. In general, cells that perform a similar function organize into a group to form a tissue. In turn, one or more tissues that perform a specific set of functions organize into 'organs'.

▶ *Epithelial cells form the outermost protective layer of skin*

▼ *Different muscle tissue is found in different organs*

Organ Systems

One or more organs can also be grouped into an 'organ system' that is involved in one function such as digestion or respiration. It must be noted that at every level (tissue, organ, organ system) the structure is related to the function performed.

In humans, some of the major tissue types include:

Epithelial tissue: Forms the outer layer (skin) of the body

Connective tissue: Forms a support network for the organs and blood vessels

Muscle tissue: Forms the muscles capable of movement

Nervous tissue: Forms the brain and spinal cord that process information and transmit signals

Cardiac muscle   Smooth muscle   Skeletal muscle

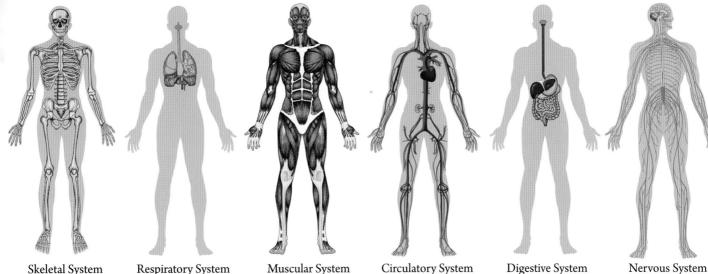

Skeletal System   Respiratory System   Muscular System   Circulatory System   Digestive System   Nervous System

▲ *Organ systems consist of organs that perform certain functions*

Organs

Organs such as heart, lungs, kidneys, liver, pancreas, are made up of tissues involved in the same function. Almost all organs contain epithelial, connective, muscular and nervous tissues. In an organ system such as the circulatory system, the heart and the blood vessels work together to pump blood to all parts of the body.

Fact File

Epithelial cells come in different shapes and are classified as cuboidal, ciliated, columnar and squamous.

13

Chromosomes and Genes

DNA forms the basic hereditary unit of a cell. It possesses all the information needed for the complete body to function. Genes code for essential proteins and are present along with non-coding segments of DNA in chromosomes.

DNA

All the information necessary for the functioning of our cells is stored in the chemical macromolecule called Deoxyribonucleic Acid or DNA. DNA is a double helix structure made up of repeating units of four nucleotides – Adenine, Guanine, Cytosine and Thymine. Each nucleotide is in turn made up of a sugar molecule, a nitrogenous base and a phosphate molecule.

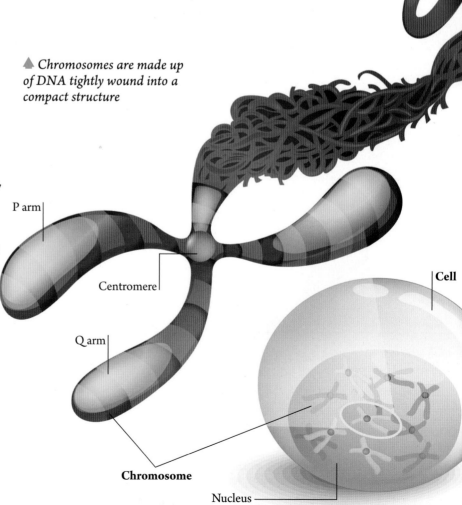

Gene

Thymine

Adenine

Guanine

DNA

Cytosine

Nucleosomes

All functions of the DNA, such as making copies of itself through replication and forming RNA through transcription are dependent on interaction with different proteins.

▲ *Chromosomes are made up of DNA tightly wound into a compact structure*

P arm

Centromere

Q arm

Cell

Chromosome

Nucleus

Genes

A gene is defined as the functional and physical unit of heredity. A gene, made up of a specific DNA sequence, acts as the instruction blueprint for making a protein. A person gets two copies of the same gene from their parents. A typical human has 20,000 to 25,000 genes coding for different proteins and responsible for various functions necessary for survival and reproduction.

Different forms of the same gene are called 'alleles'. A person inherits an allele from each parent and the combination of the alleles result in a particular feature. For instance, a person's eye colour depends on the combined effect of the two alleles inherited from the parents.

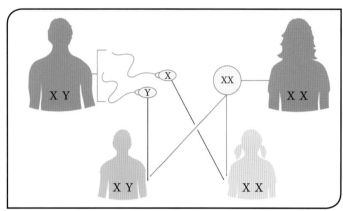

▲ *A segment of DNA wrapped around 8 histone proteins make up a nucleosome*

Chromosomes

The DNA present in a single cell stretches out to about 2 metres. The only way to fit the DNA into the tiny nucleus within a cell is to pack the DNA into compact structures called chromosomes by binding with proteins called histones. Chromosomes are usually not visible under a microscope, unless a cell is undergoing cell division.

It is during this time that the chromosomes are tightly packed and visible. A chromosome has a short 'p' arm and a long 'q' arm. The presence of a centromere in the center of the chromosome gives it its characteristic 'X' shape.

▲ *In humans, the XX-XY chromosome determines sex*

Genetic Disorders

Diseases and disorders can occur due to many reasons, but genetic disorders are caused by one or more faulty genes in a person's cells. Some disorders are caused by 'recessive' alleles. This means that a person will get the disease only if they inherit faulty copies of the genes from both parents. Cystic fibrosis is an example of a recessive genetic disorder.

'X' linked disorders are those associated with genes in the 'X' chromosome. Since females have two copies of 'X' chromosomes, two faulty copies from both parents is needed to cause the disease. On the other hand, a male will get the disease even if one 'X' chromosome has a faulty gene as there isn't an equivalent gene in the 'Y' chromosome to compensate for it. Red green colour blindness and hemophilia are examples of X-linked genetic disorders.

Sex Determination

Sex determination can vary across the plant and animal kingdom as does the number of chromosomes. In humans, the chromosomes determine the sex of the person. The body cells have 23 pairs of chromosomes each. Of the 46 chromosomes, males have one 'X' and one 'Y' chromosome whereas females have 2 'X' chromosomes.

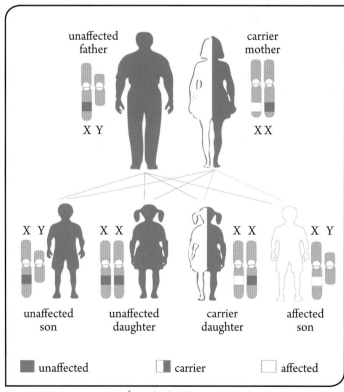

▲ *X-linked recessive inheritance disorders affect males more than females*

Fact File

If it is possible to remove the DNA present in all the cells of an adult human and place it end to end, it will stretch to at least 6000 million miles!

15

Genetic Engineering

Scientists can now isolate genes from one species and insert them into the genome of another species by a process called genetic engineering. This technique has immense potential to address many of our needs but, considering the fact that genetic engineering is equivalent to meddling with nature, it is also controversial.

By definition, the introduction of foreign genes in an organism's genome or altering specific genes through certain techniques is called genetic engineering.

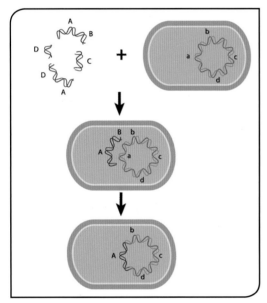

▲ *Bacterial cells accept foreign DNA through a process called 'transformation'*

Steps in Genetic Engineering

The major steps in genetic engineering using bacteria are:

Cutting out desired gene/DNA: Specific enzymes called 'restriction' enzymes, found in bacteria, are used in genetic engineering for cutting out specific DNA sequences of interest.

Insertion in vector: The isolated DNA segment is introduced into bacteria that are referred to as 'vectors'. The desired DNA is usually inserted into a plasmid, which is the bacteria's extra-chromosomal DNA. The plasmids readily accept DNA inserts and replicate inside the host bacteria and transfer the new genes across generations when the bacterium divides.

Gene replication: When the host bacteria reproduce, the plasmids also replicate and make multiple copies of the inserted segment.

Recovery: Bacterial cells that contain the plasmid with the desired DNA segment are selectively isolated from the culture.

 Fact File

'Pharming' is a gene altering technology that uses plants and animals to produce useful proteins and drugs.

Applications of Genetic Engineering

Some of the products/applications are:

• Many drugs and compounds have been mass-produced such as insulin, growth hormones, albumin, vaccines, monoclonal antibodies and anti-hemophilic factors

• Genetically engineered animal models are used for research on human diseases including arthritis, diabetes, Parkinson's disease and heart disease.

• 'Gene Therapy' is a process of inserting genes into a patient to compensate for the faulty or missing genes that cause a disease. Already, trials have been carried out for certain diseases and it shows great promise for curing many others.

◀ *Flavr Savr tomatoes remain firm for a longer duration*

• Genetic engineering is used on an industrial scale for mass production of food supplements and bio fuels.

• Production of genetically modified organisms and plants is possible through genetic engineering. Some examples of Genetically Modified Crops (GMOs) include Flavr Savr tomatoes that remain firm for a long time, golden rice that is enriched with Vitamin A and Bt Cotton resistant to a bacterial pest.

• Genetically engineered farm animals can increase yields; for example, cows can produce more proteins in their milk for increased cheese production.

▲ *Genetically engineered animal models help in studying different diseases*

▲ *Genetically modified examines a GM crop for desired features*

Concerns of Genetic Engineering

• Genetically modified crop plants that have resistance to pesticides and herbicides can affect the natural ecological balance.

• Despite precautions, there is the danger of genetically-engineered organisms spreading to the wild. Once it occurs, it is impossible to repair the damage.

• On moral grounds, many people argue that humans should not meddle with nature and do not have the right to alter or introduce traits in organisms.

• It is possible to create potentially harmful organisms through recombinant DNA technology and cause serious epidemics if released into the environment.

• Due to commercial interests, many products are not labeled 'genetically modified food'. Even if they are labeled, the ingredients are not revealed to the general public.

• There is also opposition on patents on animals, plants and organisms on the grounds that life forms are not commodities.

Cloning

Cloning is the process by which one living organism can make an exact copy of itself. The offspring is not only physically identical to the parent, but has an identical genome as well. Interestingly, the word 'clone' is borrowed from the Greek word 'klon' which means 'twig' to refer to the process of a new plant arising from a twig.

Cloning in Plants

Cloning occurs naturally in plants in different ways through asexual reproduction:

• Potato plants produce tubers which can grow roots and shoots and develop into new plants

• Spider plants have tiny plantlets growing on their stems

• Strawberry plants have stems that creep on the ground, called runners, that have plantlets on them

There are also artificial means through which plants can be cloned:

Cuttings: A branch from a parent plant is cut off and after the lower leaves are removed, it is planted in moist compost in a warm environment. In a few weeks' time, roots develop and a new plant grows.

Tissue Culture: A piece of a plant's tissue or a seed can be grown in the laboratory under artificial light and heat conditions in a 'nutrient gel' called 'medium' designed to be similar to soil. This method is known as tissue culture. Usually, plant hormones are used to encourage the cells to divide and differentiate into roots and shoots.

▲ *Plant tissue culture is relatively easier than animal culture in lab conditions*

Advantages

• Cloning provides a way to produce plants in bulk quantities otherwise difficult to grow only with seeds.

• Since all plants grown through cloning are identical, the grower can choose plants with best qualities for cloning.

Disadvantages

• Since all plants thus grown are identical, there is no diversity. As a result, if a disease affects one plant, it is likely to affect all other plants.

• High levels of training and expensive lab equipment are required for successful plant tissue culture.

Cloning in Animals

Embryo Transplants: In this technique, a developing embryo is removed from the uterus of an animal at the initial stage when the embryo has not yet specialized. The cells of the embryo are separated and grown in the laboratory and then transferred to hosts.

Assisted Nuclear Transfer: An adult cell can be cloned through the nuclear transfer method. A special tool is used in the laboratory to suck out the nucleus of the egg cell. Then the nucleus of another cell is transferred into the egg. An electric shock is given to induce division. The dividing embryo is then implanted in the uterus of the female. The developed embryo will then be a 'clone' or 'exact copy' of the parent whose nucleus was transferred.

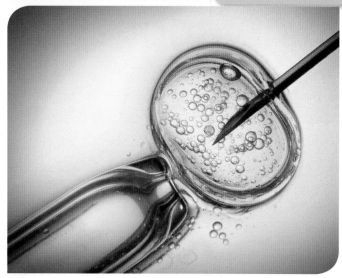

▲ *The assisted nuclear transfer is done under a powerful microscope and special equipment*

▲ *The creation of Dolly through cloning created a revolution in genetic engineering*

Dolly

In 1996, Dolly the sheep became the first mammal to be born through cloning from an adult cell. Dolly was created through the nuclear transfer technique at Roslin Institute, University of Edinburgh.

Fact File

Dolly was born after 276 failed attempts to clone a sheep.

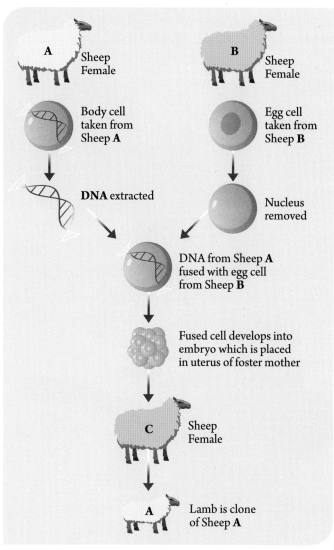

▲ *A cloned sheep resembles the parent that donates the DNA*

Advantages

• It is possible to mass produce animals with desirable characteristics, such as cows with high milk production capacity.

• Cloning can produce genetically engineered animals that can provide useful products.

Disadvantages

• The major challenges for cloning are the moral and ethical issues relating to how much humans should interfere in the production of life.

Microscopy

Microscopy is the field of science that deals with the use of instruments called microscopes to magnify objects and microbes that are not normally visible to the naked eye. The optical microscope is one of the most basic devices used for observing microbes while electron microscopes provide very high magnification.

Origin of Microscopy

Anton van Leeuwenhoek, a Dutch businessman and scientist is often considered as the 'Father of Microbiology'. He created more than 500 different optical lenses and extensively studied different samples and meticulously noted down the bacteria, cell vacuole, sperm cell and a close-up view of muscle fibers. The original lenses that Leeuwenhoek designed were very small and had to be in front of sunlight to view samples.

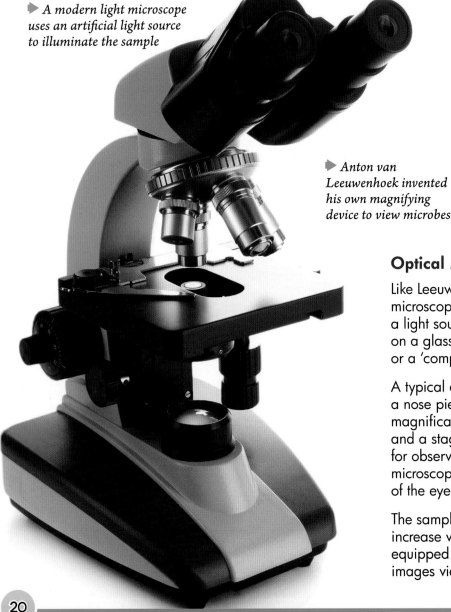

▶ *A modern light microscope uses an artificial light source to illuminate the sample*

▶ *Anton van Leeuwenhoek invented his own magnifying device to view microbes*

Optical Microscope

Like Leeuwenhoek's magnifying device, an optical microscope employs lenses and requires sunlight or a light source to illuminate the sample that is loaded on a glass slide. It is also called a 'light microscope' or a 'compound microscope'.

A typical optical microscope consists of an eyepiece, a nose piece with changeable lenses (of varying magnification power), objective lenses, light source and a stage (where the glass slide is placed for observation). The magnification power of a microscope is the combination of the magnification of the eyepiece and objective lenses.

The sample is loaded on a slide with suitable dyes to increase visibility. Modern optical microscopes are equipped with photographic plates to capture the images viewed.

Magnification and Resolution

Magnification of a device is its ability to make things appear larger. The total magnification achieved through a microscope is calculated using the following formula:

$$\text{Magnification} = \frac{\text{Size of magnified image}}{\text{Actual size of object}}$$

If you are viewing a microbe whose actual size is 1 micron (1×10^{-6} metre) and under a microscope it measures 1 millimetre (1×10^{-3} metre), then the magnification is 1000X.

At a magnification of 400X, you will be able to clearly view many species of bacteria, blood cells and protozoa. At a higher magnification, say 1000X, you'll be able to see them in much better detail. For instance, you will be able to distinguish the organelles in protozoa and see the flagella of bacteria.

A microscope's resolution is the shortest distance between two points on a specimen that can be easily distinguished as separate objects by the viewer.

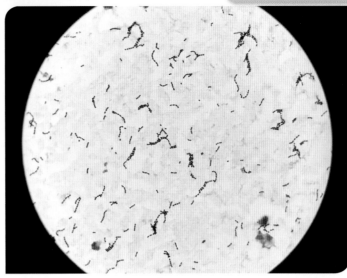

▲ *A view of stained bacteria seen under a light microscope*

 Fact File

On an average, an optical microscope can offer magnification ranging from 5 to 100X the object's original size.

◀ *Cellulose fibers of plant seen through a powerful scanning electron microscope*

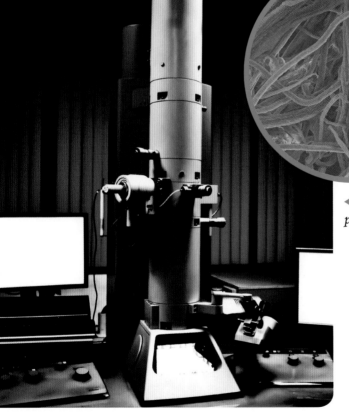

◀ *An electron microscope is large, powerful and expensive*

Other Microscopes

There are many other advanced microscopes in use. This includes the Scanning Tunneling Microscope, Phase Contrast Microscope, Fluorescence Microscope and Atomic Force Microscope that has helped view microbes and cellular features in better detail.

Electron Microscope

An electron microscope, as the name suggests, uses a stream of electrons instead of visible light to provide the magnification. As a result, very high magnification, in the range of 100,000 to 200,000X is possible with this microscope. Unlike light microscopes, live samples cannot be used directly. The samples are processed to remove water, embedded in a resin, cut into thin slices and stained suitably for viewing in an electron microscope. With an electron microscope, it is possible to view cell organelles, viruses that are extremely small, in the range of nanometres (1 nanometre = 1×10^{-9} metre) and even individual atoms. Electron microscopes are expensive to construct and maintain. Those who operate it need special training to handle it with care.

Growing Microbes in the Lab

Different species of microbes grow on different substrates. To study and understand microorganisms they are grown under the right conditions in the laboratory using specifically designed artificial substrate called 'medium'. Bacteria are the easiest and most common microbes to be artificially grown.

Reproduction

Bacteria grow rapidly through a method of asexual reproduction called 'binary fission'. In binary fission, the duplication of the genetic material of a bacterial cell is followed by cell elongation and division to form two separate cells. This method of reproduction is very simple compared to that of cell division in eukaryotes.

◀ Bacteria reproduce through binary fission

Growing Bacterial Culture

In the laboratory, bacteria are grown in a specific chemical medium to produce 'colonies'. It was the biologist, Robert Koch, who first grew bacteria in a specially designed petri dish, a technique that is still followed today. Koch had grown bacteria that caused tuberculosis and cholera. Today, many different bacteria can be cultivated and investigated in the lab.

Even though the requirements vary for different species, the common nutrient medium is a jelly-like substance called agar, derived from a type of red algae. Agar provides the ideal surface for the bacteria to grow and produce colonies. The agar is enriched with nutrients like beef or yeast extract to provide amino acids and nitrogen needed for the growth of bacteria.

▶ Bacteria are grown in special liquid growth medium in the lab

▲ A laminar air flow cabinet offers the ideal environment for safely working with microbes

Requirements for Growing Bacteria

In order to encourage the growth of bacteria in a laboratory, the whole process of transferring bacterial culture from a solution to the petri dish is done under sterile conditions, typically in a laminar air flow cabin, with the work area swabbed with alcohol. The nutrient agar is allowed to solidify in a sterilized petri dish. 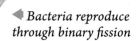 Samples are collected from soil, air, surfaces or body fluids and diluted in water.

An inoculation loop is used for transferring bacteria from a solution to the agar. It is sterilized by exposure to flame before use. The loop, dipped in bacterial solution, is then gently rubbed over the agar quickly and sealed with tape.

Incubation

The process by which bacteria inoculated in the petri dishes are stored under suitable conditions is called 'incubation'. Since bacteria reproduce quickly in warm conditions, they are stored at an optimum temperature of 25°C.

▲ *A sterilised inoculation loop is used for transferring microbes to a petri dish*

Bacterial Colonies

Different species of bacteria produce different colonies varying in colour, shape and texture. If the same petri dish has two different colonies, studying the morphology of the colonies helps identify the bacteria species.

◀ *Different bacterial species form different colonies*

Fact File

Petri dishes are generally never incubated at room temperature (37°C) as many harmful bacteria that can cause diseases grow and flourish in this temperature range.

Testing for Antibiotics and Disinfectants

One of the useful functions of culturing microorganisms is to identify the efficiency of an antibiotic, disinfectant or any anti-bacterial substance. For this, the bacteria are inoculated evenly across the entire petri dish with a swab or inoculation loop. Then a drop of the anti-bacterial substance or an antibiotic disc is placed in the centre of the dish and incubated. The presence of a 'halo' surrounding the anti-bacterial substance shows a region of no growth of bacteria around it. The diameter of the halo also indicates the efficiency of the antibiotic/anti-bacterial agent.

Disposal

Petri dishes with bacterial culture must be disposed of carefully to avoid contamination. Gloves are worn when handling petri dishes with bacterial colonies and bleach is poured over the agar to destroy the bacterial growth before disposal.

Diseases

Health is the state of well-being whereas a disease or disorder is an affliction that affects one or more parts of the body. Diseases can be of different types and can be caused by infection, poor lifestyle, genetic predisposition, deficiency or other factors. The most common classification of diseases is communicable or non-communicable.

Non-communicable Diseases

Diseases that cannot be spread from one person to another through physical contact or exposure are known as non-communicable diseases. Some of the common examples of non-communicable diseases are

Diabetes: It is caused by high blood sugar levels or deficiency of insulin

Cancer: It is a result of abnormal growth and division of cells

Cardiac arrest: Blockages in the heart's blood vessels cause heart attack

Stroke: Changes in the blood supply to the brain can result in a stroke

Asthma: A disease that affects lungs and causes difficulty breathing

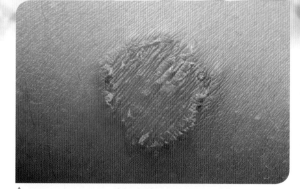

▲ *Ringworm is a skin infection caused by a fungal species*

Communicable Diseases

Diseases that can spread from one person to another through different means are termed as communicable diseases. The mode of spreading varies from one disease to another as does the severity. The common cold is a relatively mild condition caused by bacteria or viruses whereas smallpox is a severe and sometimes deadly disease caused by a virus.

The disease spreads from one person to another through air, water, soil, animals, birds, insects, body fluids or sexual contact.

- Diseases caused by Bacteria: Sore throat, tuberculosis, gonorrhea, pneumonia

- Diseases caused by Protists: Sleeping sickness, Chagas disease, Malaria

- Diseases caused by Fungi: Ringworm, Psoriasis, Yeast infections

- Diseases caused by Viruses: Chickenpox, Polio, Measles, Hepatitis, Influenza

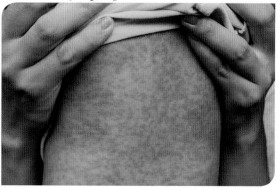

▲ *Measles is a viral infection that affects children*

Risk factors

Both communicable and non-communicable diseases are caused by certain aspects and lifestyle choices that may increase the chance of the person acquiring the disease. They are known as 'risk factors'. Some risk factors associated with both types of diseases include:

- Poor hygiene
- Lack of exercise
- Unhealthy diet
- Deficiency of vitamins or minerals
- Excessive consumption of alcohol
- Smoking cigarettes
- Obesity

- Exposure to harmful chemicals, radiation or cancer-causing agents (carcinogens)
- Genetic factors, as in the case of inherited diseases
- Lack of, or poor functioning of, one or more components

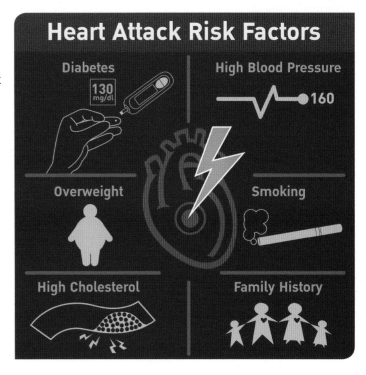

Heart Attack Risk Factors

Diabetes
130 mg/dl

High Blood Pressure
160

Overweight

Smoking

High Cholesterol

Family History

Diseases in Plants

Diseases can affect plants too. These diseases are caused by microbes like fungi, bacteria, viruses and also insects. Plants exhibit different symptoms corresponding to the disease as spots, stunted growth, decay, cankers, malformed leaves or stems, and discolouration.

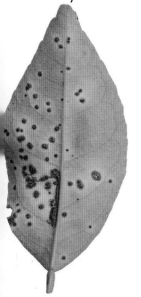

▲ *Citrus canker in leaves of lemon tree exhibit brown, raised spots*

◀ *Some stems have thorns to protect against animals*

Defense Mechanisms

Plants have different defense mechanisms to protect against herbivores and diseases. They are:

- Thick cell walls
- Waxy and tough cuticle on leaves
- Dead cells around stems in the form of bark
- Secretion of chemical compounds
- Secretion of poisonous substances
- Thorns and hairs
- Mimicry
- Leaves that curl or droop when touched

Fact File

Communicable diseases are caused by infection of microbes such as bacteria, fungi, protists and viruses that are referred to as 'pathogens'.

Immunity

Immunity is the ability of the body to fight against foreign agents like microbes that enter into the body. The human body has its own natural immune system but when it isn't sufficient, there are other ways to prevent or treat certain diseases through artificial methods.

Natural Immunity

Our body has certain non-specific defense systems that try and keep out dust and pathogens from entering into the body. The skin is one of the first layers of defense. The nose has hairs and mucus to trap and filter out microbes and dirt. The ear has a waxy secretion that performs a similar function. The mouth has saliva that has anti-microbial properties.

The body's innate immune system consists of many different immune cells that have receptors for detecting foreign agents like bacteria, viruses or anything else. Once it binds to it, the cell destroys the pathogen or foreign particle in a process called phagocytosis. Neutrophils and macrophages are examples of phagocytic cells.

Natural Killer Cells look for viruses as well as cancer cells and release chemicals to destroy them. Eosinophils, Neutrophils and Basophils also look out for pathogens and release enzymes to destroy them.

▼ *T-cells are immune cells that find and bind to foreign molecules and cancer cells*

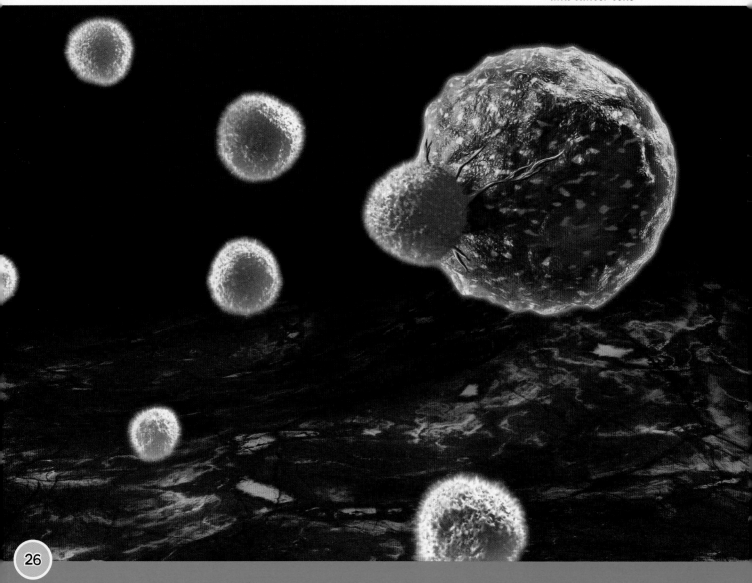

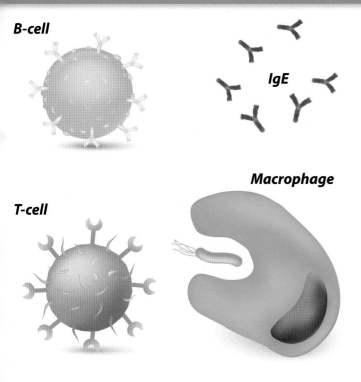

B-cell

IgE

Macrophage

T-cell

T-cells and B-cells are the two types of immune cells that make up the adaptive immune system. Unlike the innate immune system that can't differentiate one pathogen from another, the T-cells and B-cells are capable of specifically targeting and destroying them. B-cells secrete antibodies that can bind and destroy pathogens.

Dendritic cells perform a crucial function of linking the innate and adaptive immune systems. They digest foreign bodies and present their antigens (surface proteins) to the lymphocytes so that the next time the same foreign bodies are encountered, the immune system can react in a quicker and more efficient way.

◀ *Different types of immune cells perform different functions*

Artificial Immunity

Artificial immunity is conferred through vaccination to protect the person against certain diseases that are dangerous such as typhoid, pertussis, tetanus, diphtheria, polio and hepatitis.

Vaccinations are generally prepared by using dead or weakened microbes responsible for causing the disease and introducing it into the body. They stimulate the body's immune system to react and retain the memory of the microbe's antigens so that if the person ever comes in contact with the microbe again, the immune cells are ready to act quickly to destroy it.

Antibiotics are medicines that are used for treating certain bacterial diseases. These antibiotics are extracted from plants or fungal moulds that are toxic to bacteria. While most antibiotics target bacteria, a few can also be helpful for treating diseases caused by protists. Antibiotics are not effective against viruses.

Drugs and Monoclonal Antibodies

Apart from antibiotics, different drugs are produced to target a wide range of infections and diseases. Many drugs are synthesized artificially in laboratories and undergo several rounds of clinical testing before being introduced to the market.

Monoclonal Antibodies are produced by combining a lymphocyte with a type of cancer cell to form a hybridoma cell. This hybridoma cell is capable of dividing rapidly and producing mass quantities of a specific type of antibody. These antibodies are collected and purified to use for treating certain diseases.

Fact File

Penicillin was one of the first antibiotics developed by Alexander Fleming to fight bacterial infections. Penicillin was derived from the Penicillium mould, a type of fungus.

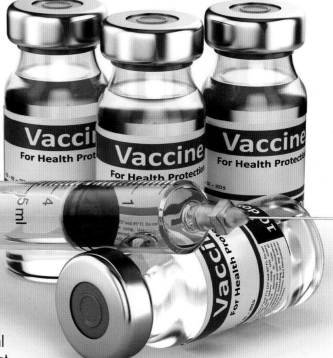

▲ *Vaccinations are administered to prevent many diseases*

Classification of Organisms

There are millions of organisms that exist on our planet. Classification is a method devised by scientists to place organisms in specific groups based on physical and biological similarities.

Though certain organisms might seem different from others, if they have enough similarities, they can be grouped into one category. This systematic method of classifying organisms is called taxonomy. Carl Linnaeus, a Swedish botanist, was responsible for classifying organisms on the basis of physical appearance and characteristics and giving a scientific name (also called binomial nomenclature) for every species.

Divisions

In taxonomic classification, organisms are sorted in a hierarchical system on the basis of these ranks or taxa:

Domain > Kingdom > Phylum > Class > Order > Family > Genus > Species

The 5 kingdom system of classification was proposed by R.H. Whittaker in 1969. Many countries follow this system of classification. The classification is based on many factors like type of nutrition, cell structure and type of reproduction.

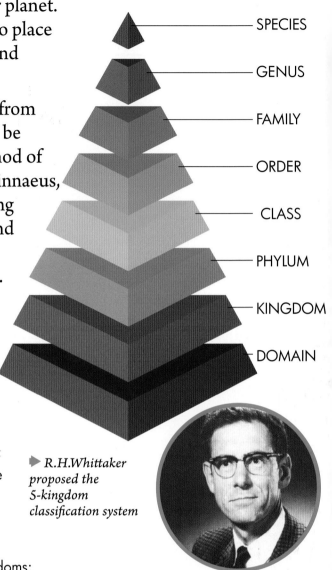

SPECIES
GENUS
FAMILY
ORDER
CLASS
PHYLUM
KINGDOM
DOMAIN

▶ *R.H.Whittaker proposed the 5-kingdom classification system*

Five Kingdom Classification

The known organisms are classified into any of the five kingdoms:

Kingdom	Characteristic Features	Examples		
Animalia	Multicellular No cell walls No pigments for photosynthesis	Chamaeleon	Sea Turtle	Chimpanzee
Plantae	Multicellular Cell walls present Photosynthetic pigments present Manufactures own food from sunlight	Ferns	Apple tree	Green Algae

Fungi	Unicellular or Multicellular Cell walls present No pigments for photosynthesis	Mushrooms Yeast Moulds
Protoctists	Unicellular Well-defined nucleus May possess pigments for photosynthesis	Green Euglena Amoeba Paramecium
Prokaryotes	Unicellular Cell walls present Primitive/not-well defined nucleus May have extra-chromosomal DNA called 'plasmids'	Bacteria Archaebacteria Cyanobacteria

An example of how humans would be classified in this system:

Classification	Name	Reason
Domain	Eukaryotes	Possesses well-defined nucleus
Kingdom	Animalia	Multicellular, capable of ingesting food, no cell walls
Phylum	Chordata	Presence of backbone
Class	Mammalia	Give birth to live young ones, nurse offspring with milk
Order	Primates	High level of intelligence; ape-like
Family	Hominidae	Capable of walking upright
Genus	Homo	Human
Species	sapiens	Modern day human

The classification system is an indication of the evolutionary relationship between organisms. All living beings classified under a phylum, for example Chordata, are assumed to have evolved from a common ancestor.

Fact File

No classification system includes viruses in any group because they are not considered to be true living organisms.

▶ *Human species are thought to have evolved from a common 'ape' ancestor*

Bioenergetics: Photosynthesis

Plants, algae and certain species of bacteria can directly use sunlight to make their own food in the form of simple sugars. This process is known as photosynthesis, where photo means 'light' and synthesis means 'putting together'. Photosynthesis requires special cell organelles and pigments.

Photosynthesis Process

Plants can perform 'photosynthesis' to make their own food by using sunlight, water and carbon dioxide. Sunlight is absorbed by a type of green pigment in the cells called 'chlorophyll'. Water is absorbed from the soil and air through the roots and leaves. Carbon dioxide is taken in through small pores on leaves called 'stomata'.

Oxygen

Sunlight

Carbon Dioxide

Minerals

Water

▲ *Green leaves have chloroplasts that perform photosynthesis*

▲ *Sunlight, water and air are essential for plants to survive and make their food*

Chlorophyll pigment is located within the cells in organelles called 'chloroplasts'. It is this pigment that is responsible for the green colour of leaves. Chlorophyll is capable of absorbing sun's energy and uses it to split the water molecules into hydrogen and oxygen.

Even leaves of other colours perform photosynthesis. Leaves can be red or yellow in colour due to the presence of different pigments like anthocyanin, carotene or xanthophyll. Even coloured leaves possess chlorophyll to perform photosynthesis.

While oxygen is released into the atmosphere as a byproduct, hydrogen then combines with carbon dioxide to produce a simple sugar called 'glucose'. Glucose molecules are used for providing energy for the growth and development of the plants. The rest of it is stored in the leaves, roots and fruits.

The chemical reaction can be written as:

Carbon dioxide + Water $\xrightarrow{\text{Sunlight}}$ Glucose + Oxygen

$$CO_2 + H_2O \xrightarrow{\text{Sunlight}} C_6H_{12}O_6 + O_2$$

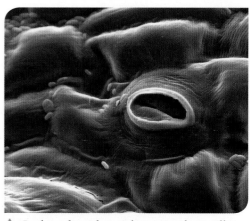

▲ *Carbon dioxide is taken into plant cells through stomata opening*

Light Reaction: This reaction occurs in the thylakoid membrane of chloroplasts and requires sunlight. This is the process by which light energy is converted into chemical energy. The water molecule is broken down into ions (H+ and OH-). These ions help form the molecules - ATP (Adenosine Tri Phosphate) and NADPH2 (Nicotinamide Adenine Dinucleotide Phosphate). These two molecules are used in the next stage.

Dark Reaction: In the second step, no light is required. This is a slower reaction that uses enzymes to synthesize sugars from carbon dioxide and water with the help of the energy molecules, ATP and NADPH2. This stage is also known as 'carbon fixation' or the Calvin Cycle.

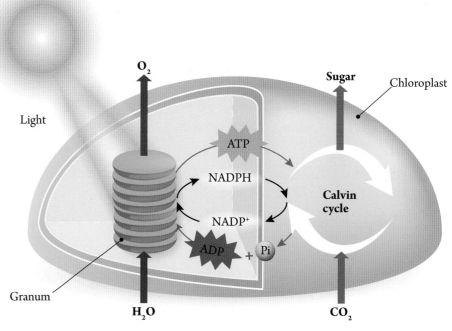

▲ *The light reaction occurs through a series of steps*

Importance of Photosynthesis

Photosynthesis sustains life on Earth. Plants use the glucose created for growth and energy. Animals then consume plants for energy needs and survival. The animals that feed on plants are known as primary consumers or herbivores. Photosynthesis facilitates respiration for animals because the oxygen produced by the plants is used for respiration. Photosynthesis is therefore directly related to the life and survival of all living creatures on earth.

Coal and natural gas are products of dead and buried plant material from millions of years ago. We use these fossil fuels for generating electricity.

Fact File

Photosynthesis is essential for balancing the levels of carbon dioxide and oxygen on the planet.

▲ *Coal is formed from dead remains of plants that died millions of years ago*

▶ *Fossil fuels form under the surface from buried parts of plants and animals*

Bioenergetics: Respiration, Metabolism and Homeostasis

Biochemical processes like respiration, metabolism and homeostasis are vital for survival of organisms. They occur continuously in healthy, living cells and enable production of energy, effective utilization of the energy produced and maintenance of constant body temperature and pressure.

Metabolism

The cells in the body convert fuel obtained from the food that is consumed and convert it into energy required for performing all functions. This process is known as metabolism. In a human body, different proteins control the chemical reactions of metabolism in a coordinated manner. At any given time, thousands of metabolic reactions are occurring inside the body.

The sugars produced by plants through photosynthesis are consumed by animals. These sugars are broken down into important cell-building chemical components. Metabolism has two functions:

1) It helps build up body tissues and energy reserves

2) It breaks down energy stores and body tissues to generate fuel for functioning.

Metabolism is of two types:

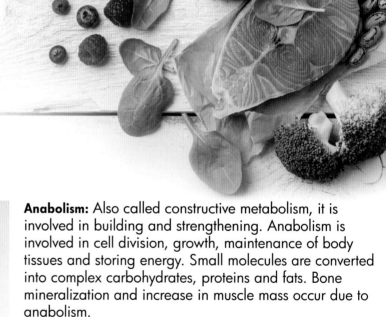

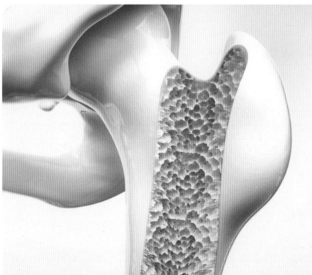

Anabolism: Also called constructive metabolism, it is involved in building and strengthening. Anabolism is involved in cell division, growth, maintenance of body tissues and storing energy. Small molecules are converted into complex carbohydrates, proteins and fats. Bone mineralization and increase in muscle mass occur due to anabolism.

Catabolism: Also known as destructive metabolism, it is a process that generates energy for cellular activities in the cells. Cells break down complex carbohydrates and fats to release energy. This release of energy is followed by increase in body heat and muscular movement. The waste products of catabolism are removed through the kidneys, skin, intestines or lungs.

🔺 *Bone mineralisation occurs through anabolism*

Respiration

Cellular respiration is a process that breaks up sugar into energy molecules. Respiration can be either aerobic (when it uses oxygen) or anaerobic (when oxygen is not required). Anaerobic respiration is not as efficient as aerobic respiration and also produces carbon dioxide as a byproduct which then gains entry into the circulatory system. Mitochondria are organelles in the cell that facilitate respiration.

Respiration consists of four stages:

- Glycolysis

- Link Reaction

- Krebs Cycle

- Electron Transport Chain

Aerobic respiration can be represented by the formula:

Glucose + Oxygen $\longrightarrow$ Carbon dioxide + Water + Energy

$$C_6H_{12}O_6 + 6O_2 \longrightarrow 6CO_2 + 6H_2O + ATP$$

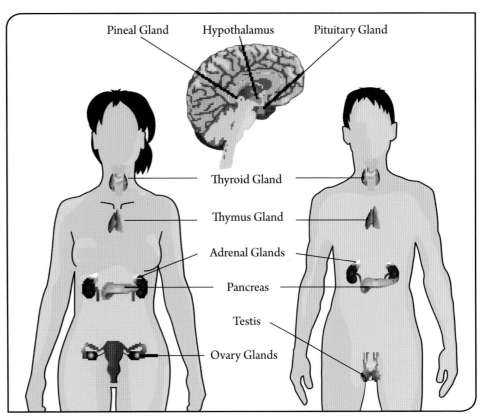

PHOTOSYNTHESIS

$CO_2 + H_2O$

Light energy

Chloroplast

$C_6H_{12}O_6 + O_2$

CELL RESPIRATION

Mitochondria

Chemical energy (ATP)

▶ *Photosynthesis and respiration enable life on Earth*

Fact File

Approximately, 29 to 30 ATP molecules are produced through oxidation of one glucose molecule. The theoretical estimate is 38 ATPs.

Homeostasis

Homeostasis refers to the body processes involved in maintaining the optimal conditions in the body for the cells to function effectively. It includes keeping the body temperature, blood glucose and water at the right levels.

To achieve the optimal conditions, the control systems involve nervous and chemical responses such as cell receptors that detect stimuli, coordination centers like brain and spinal cord that can process information and effectors that elicit the response such as muscles and glands.

There are different ways by which the human body maintains homeostasis. Body temperature is one of the most important factors that is regulated for optimal functioning of the body. When the body temperature rises in response to hot weather, the body reacts by sweating to cool down the temperature. The internal organs like lungs, pancreas and kidneys help maintain ideal levels of oxygen, blood sugar and ions. The endocrine system secretes different hormones that maintain homeostasis in the body.

Pineal Gland   Hypothalamus   Pituitary Gland

Thyroid Gland

Thymus Gland

Adrenal Glands

Pancreas

Testis

Ovary Glands

▲ *The endocrine system maintains homeostasis in the body*

Human Systems

The human body is complex and involves seamless coordination of tissues and organ systems to ensure that all activities from movement, respiration, circulation, coordination, digestion and excretion are carried out efficiently.

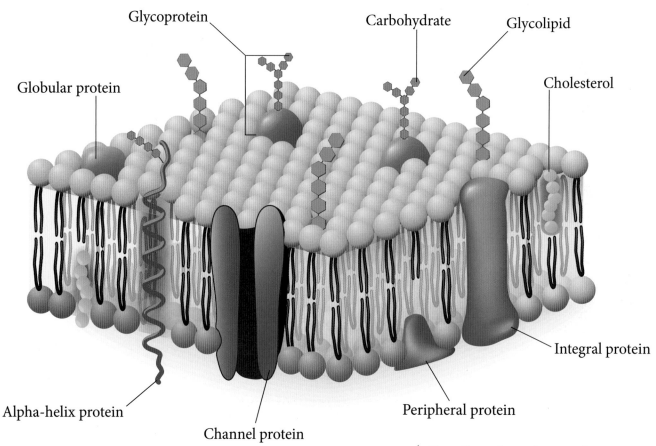

Glycoprotein

Carbohydrate

Glycolipid

Globular protein

Cholesterol

Alpha-helix protein

Channel protein

Peripheral protein

Integral protein

▲ *The cell membrane is a complex structure made of fat and protein molecules*

Chemical Composition

The cells of the human body are made-up of carbohydrates, proteins, lipids (fats), nucleic acids, organic compounds, minerals and water. Water is a major constituent in extracellular fluids such as blood, plasma and lymph and is also found within the cells. By weight, water makes up 60 percent of the human body.

Lipids, especially the phospholipids and cholesterol, form the structural component of the cells in the body, act as energy reserves, and provide insulation and shock absorption. Proteins also form the structural framework of cell membranes and enzymes are proteins that are crucial for many functions.

Carbohydrates, in the form of sugars, mainly serve as a source of fuel. Nucleic acids are the genetic material of the body that carries all the information needed for survival and reproduction. The minerals and other organic compounds play different important roles within the body.

 Fact File

The larynx, or the voice box, consists of a flap of elastic cartilage called epiglottis that makes sure that food and air go to the right destinations.

The Different Systems

Systems are the highest and most complex working units of the human body. The major systems of the human body are: Nervous, Skeletal and Muscular, Cardiovascular, Lymphatic, Respiratory, Digestive, Reproductive and Excretory.

Skeletal and Muscular System

The skeleton and the different groups of muscles form the structural framework of the body and enable movement. Cartilage and bones are the structural components of the skeletal system. The bones, apart from providing a structural framework, also store minerals such as calcium and phosphate. The bone marrow is the site for production of red blood cells. The human skeletal system has a total of 206 bones.

The muscular system is the largest system in the body and is located throughout all regions from head to toe. The three types of muscles are: cardiac, skeletal and smooth.

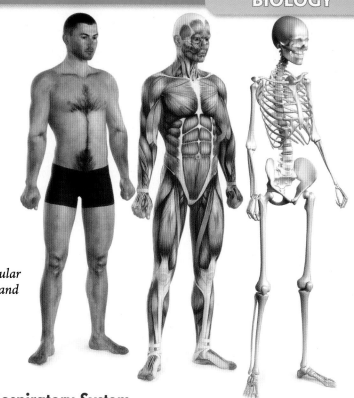

▶ *The skeletal and muscular system provides support and enables movement*

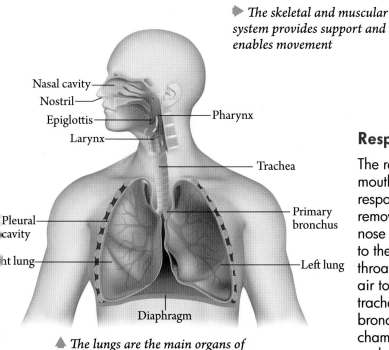

Nasal cavity
Nostril
Epiglottis
Larynx
Pharynx
Trachea
Primary bronchus
Pleural cavity
ht lung
Left lung
Diaphragm

▲ *The lungs are the main organs of respiration*

Respiratory System

The respiratory system which comprises the nose, mouth, pharynx, larynx, lungs, trachea and alveoli, is responsible for supplying the body with oxygen and removing carbon dioxide produced in the body. The nose or the nasal cavity breathes in air that is taken to the lungs. The pharynx, also referred to as the throat, is a muscular pathway that transports food and air to the larynx. From the larynx, air moves into the trachea or the wind pipe. The trachea branches into bronchial tubes and bronchioles that lead into the lung chambers. The lungs have alveoli that take up oxygen and expel carbon dioxide.

Reproductive System

The male and female reproductive systems are distinct. The male reproductive system is responsible for the production of the sperm cells that are delivered into the female's reproductive tract. The sperm is produced in the testes and travel through the penis. The eggs are produced in the ovaries in a female and travel down the fallopian tubes. When a sperm fuses with an egg cell, it gets embedded in the uterus to divide and develop into a fetus.

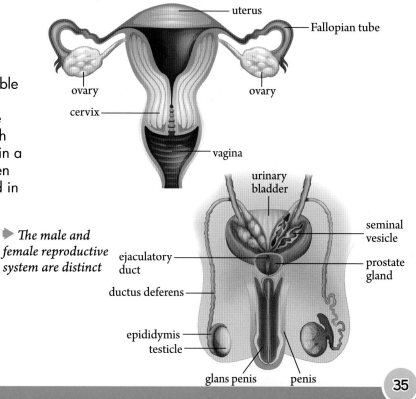

uterus
Fallopian tube
ovary
ovary
cervix
vagina
urinary bladder
seminal vesicle
ejaculatory duct
prostate gland
ductus deferens
epididymis
testicle
glans penis
penis

▶ *The male and female reproductive system are distinct*

Integumentary System

It is commonly known as the 'skin' and covers the entire body and offers protection and temperature regulation. The skin also hosts millions of nerves that respond to external stimuli like pressure, pain, touch and temperature.

35

Nervous System

Considered to be the main controlling and communicating system in the body, the nervous system controls all our actions, thoughts and emotions. Even though it is a single system, it is divided into the Central Nervous System comprising of the brain and spinal cord as well as the Peripheral Nervous System that includes the nerves that extend from the brain and spinal cord – the cranial and spinal nerves respectively. The brain is enclosed in a protective covering called cranium or the brain box.

Immune System

The skin forms the first line of defense, acting as a physical barrier against pathogens and harmful substances. The lymphatic system is responsible for fighting bacteria and fungi. Inside the body, the lymphatic system consists of the T-cells, B-cells, antibodies and platelets that tackle wound sites. While platelets repair the wound, the B-cells produce antibodies that bind to pathogens and enable the T-cells to attack them.

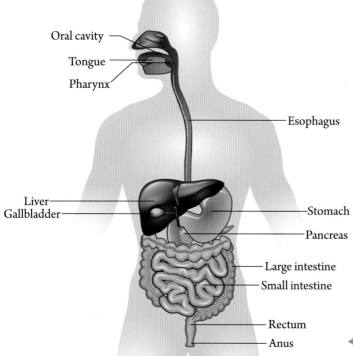

Oral cavity
Tongue
Pharynx
Esophagus
Liver
Gallbladder
Stomach
Pancreas
Large intestine
Small intestine
Rectum
Anus

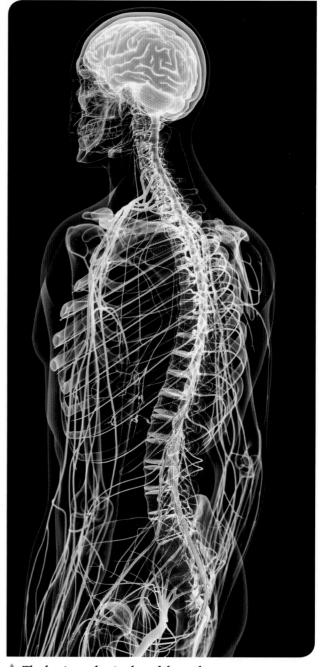

▲ *The brain and spinal cord form the nervous system*

◀ *The digestive system begins in the mouth and ends at the anus*

Digestive System

Digestion starts in the mouth and ends at the anus. The food we eat through the mouth, is mixed with saliva, broken down into pieces and passed through the alimentary canal, all the way to the stomach where many enzymes are present. The food is then broken down into simpler nutrients – proteins are broken down into amino acids, carbohydrates are converted into simple sugars and fats are converted into fatty acids. Digestion continues in the small intestine and the large intestine where nutrients are absorbed and the waste products are eliminated through the anus as feces.

Fact File

Mucous membrane lines the openings in the body acting as another barrier against foreign bodies.

Excretory System

The waste products produced in our body after digestion are expelled as urine. The kidneys are the major organs involved in excreting wastes and purifying blood. The urinary bladder, ureters and urethra form the urinary system that expels the urine produced in the kidneys. The bladder is a hollow muscular sac that can hold urine. The kidneys are bean-shaped organs enclosed by transparent and fibrous renal capsules.

Endocrine System

The endocrine system regulates different metabolic functions in the body through hormones. The hormones are chemical compounds released into the bloodstream, and tissues respond to the hormones in specific ways. The organs of the endocrine system are small. They include the pituitary gland, the thyroid and parathyroid glands, adrenal gland, pineal gland and the thymus. Hormones are of two types: steroids and amino-acid based compounds.

Circulatory System

The heart is the organ that pumps oxygen-rich blood to all parts of the body. The heart has four chambers and is made up of cardiac tissue that helps the organ pump blood. The arteries carry oxygenated blood from the heart to the other parts of the body while the veins bring deoxygenated blood from across the body back to the heart in a continuous circulatory network.

▶ Kidneys dispose waste as urine and purify blood

▶ The heart is the major pumping organ of the circulatory system

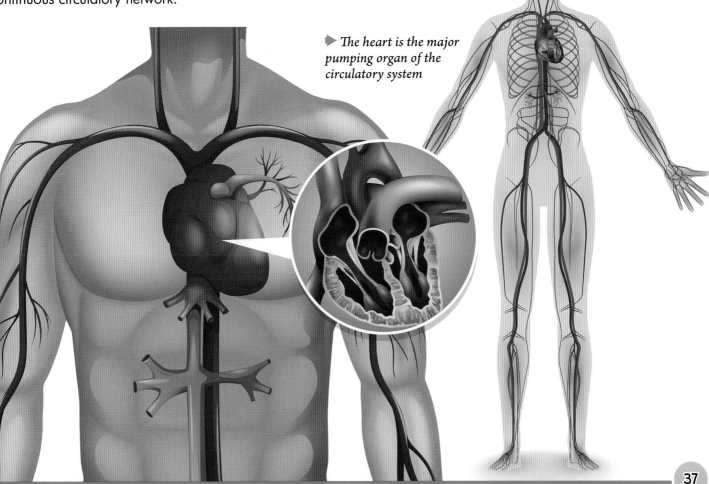

Genetics

For centuries, people have observed genetic inheritance (where offspring inherit the characteristics of their parents). This knowledge has gradually been used for improving animals and crops with favorable characteristics, but it wasn't until the nineteenth century that scientists discovered the depths of modern genetics that we are familiar with today.

History of Genetics

Imre Festetics de Tona was a pioneer of experimental genetics. He did extensive studies on sheep and was the first to propose a set of rules of heredity. He was the first to use the term 'genetic' when he wrote about the 'Genetic Laws of Nature' in 1819.

Gregor Mendel, an Austrian priest, is known as the 'Father of Modern Genetics'. He gained inspiration from his mentors and colleagues to study variations in plants. He chose the pea plant to conduct his experiments on. For eight years, starting from 1856, Mendel grew pea plants in a garden plot in the monastery and studied different traits like size and shape of seed, pod shape, flower colour, plant height and few other factors and noted down the observations.

Fact File

The Human Genome Project enabled the sequencing of the entire human genome in 2003.

Inheritance

The property by which organisms pass on heritable units called genes from one parent to offspring is known as inheritance. Gregor Mendel was the first to discover this while studying heritable traits in pea plants. One particular observation he made was how pea plants possessed either purple or white flowers but never an intermediate colour. The components that give rise to these two different colours are different versions of the same gene, called alleles. An organism with two copies of the same allele is called 'homozygous' while those having two different copies of the alleles are called 'heterozygous'. The set of alleles make up the organism's 'genotype' and the physical and observable character they result in is the 'phenotype'.

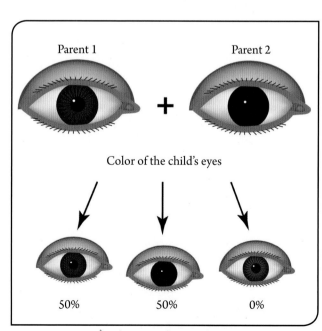

Parent 1   Parent 2

Color of the child's eyes

50%   50%   0%

▲ The eye colour is determined by alleles inherited from parents

Identification of the 'Heritable' Molecule

It wasn't until 1900 that Mendel's work gained recognition when Hugo de Vries and a few other scientists understood the significance of his experiments and research. In 1905, William Bateson, another scientist who was a strong proponent of Mendel's work, suggested the name 'genetics' to describe the study of inheritance in organisms.

Up until the early twentieth century, nobody was sure about what molecules in organisms were responsible for inheritance. Thomas Morgan Hunt identified that chromosomes were responsible for it in 1911.

However, scientists found that chromosomes were made up of proteins and DNA and nobody was sure which of the two components aided inheritance.

Experiments conducted by Griffith, Avery, MacLeod, McCarty, Hershey and Chase from 1928 to 1952 conclusively identified DNA as the genetic material.

Structure of DNA

The two scientists, James Watson and Francis Crick, with the help of X-ray crystallography pictures from Rosalind Franklin and Maurice Wilkins successfully determined the structure of DNA in 1953. DNA is a double helix, shaped like a corkscrew, with two strands of nucleotides bonded in a 'twisted ladder' fashion.

The four nucleotides in the DNA – Adenine, Guanine, Cytosine and Thymine formed complementary bonds. Adenine bonded with Thymine and Guanine with Cytosine. RNA also has four nucleotides, but with one difference – instead of Thymine, RNA has Uracil.

The process of replication occurs when the two strands of DNA are unwound and partner strands are generated by adding complementary nucleotides to both the strands thus forming two strands of which each has the original parent strand. The elucidation of the structure of DNA was followed by other discoveries, giving a clear picture of the inner molecular events.

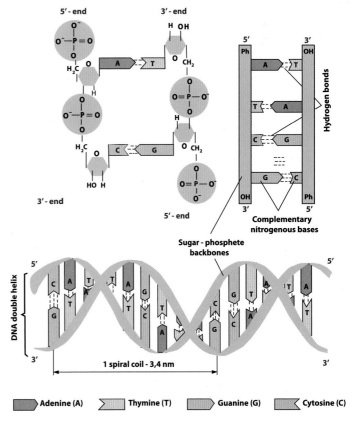

▲ *DNA is made up of molecules that form a double helix structure*

Evolution

The organisms that exist on the planet are complex, each with its own distinct features and genetic makeup. The complexity and organization are due to millions of years of evolution and the selection of the fittest for survival and propagation.

Theory of Evolution

Charles Darwin, an English naturalist, went on a 5-year voyage around the world, studying variations in plants and animals. He proposed the theory of evolution, and other ideas, in his work 'On the Origin of Species' published in 1859. The idea behind the theory of evolution is that all the different species evolved from simple, single-celled life forms. These simple organisms are believed to have first developed 3 billion years ago.

Even though Darwin's theory is more popular and widely accepted among evolutionists, he was not the only person to propose an evolution theory. A French scientist, Jean-Baptiste Lamarck developed an alternative theory in the early 19th century. His theory described that characteristics in organisms that are used more often, become bigger and stronger.

Evolutionists have noted that Lamarck's theory of evolution did not hold true for many observations on Earth. According to his theory, all organisms would evolve and become more complex over time. It did not account for the presence of simple microorganisms that have remained for billions of years.

▲ *Charles Darwin is known for his theory of evolution of species*

Natural Selection and Selective Breeding

Natural selection is a key feature of Darwin's theory of evolution. Quite simply, it means that individual species show variation, caused by differences in one or more genes. Individuals with characteristics best suited for survival are more likely to survive, reproduce and pass on the genes responsible for the beneficial characteristics.

Selective breeding is an artificial process by which humans choose desirable characteristics in animals and birds and mate them with others in their species with the same or different beneficial characteristic. As a result, the offspring will be robust and possess ideal characteristics inherited from its parents.

▲ *Quails and other birds/animals are selectively bred for best features*

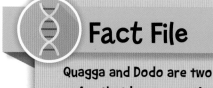

Fact File

Quagga and Dodo are two species that became extinct just a few centuries ago.

Mutation and Speciation

Mutations are changes that occur in genes that can be beneficial or harmful. These changes are also random and often caused by background radiation, chemicals and other factors. If mutations occur in the reproductive cells like sperm and ova, they get transferred to the offspring. If the mutation is beneficial and not harmful, it will continue getting transferred across generations through natural selection.

The combined effect of mutations, environmental changes and natural selection can produce enough changes in an organism to become so different that it results in the formation of a new species. This process is known as 'speciation'. The new species that has thus evolved is no longer capable of breeding and producing fertile offspring with the original species.

▲ *White tigers are a variation of Bengal tiger with different pigmentation genes*

Evidence of Evolution

Fossils: Most of the evidence for evolution came from fossils (preserved remains unearthed from Earth layers) of organisms that lived during different periods of time.

Peppered Moths: Before the Industrial Revolution in Britain, only the pale variety of peppered moths was common. The mutant moths with black colouring were at a disadvantage as they were easily spotted and eaten by birds. With an increase in pollution, the black variety moths became better camouflaged compared to their paler counterparts.

Antibiotic Resistance in Microbes: Bacteria and viruses can rapidly evolve and change their outer coats that are targeted by antibiotics, thus gaining antibiotic resistance. This happens due to beneficial mutations that offer advantage to the mutated species that, in turn, reproduce and make more copies.

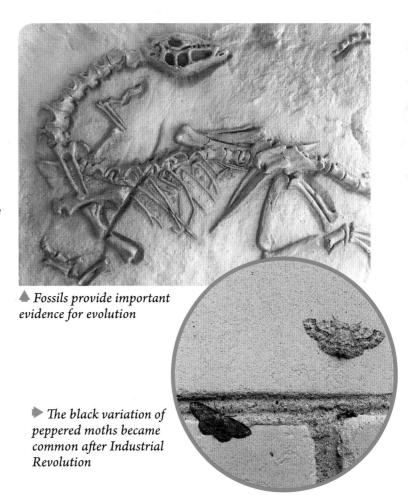

▲ *Fossils provide important evidence for evolution*

▶ *The black variation of peppered moths became common after Industrial Revolution*

◀ *Quagga is an extinct species resembling a zebra*

Extinction and Factors

Organisms become extinct due to rapid changes in climate or environment, excessive predation, new and deadly diseases and new competitors or loss of habitat. In the present, many species have become extinct, and more are critically endangered due to human activity.

Ecosystems

Ecology is a branch of science that studies the interaction between organisms and their environments. Human beings have not only played a role in threatening biodiversity, but also in taking measures to limit activities that endanger the environment and protect other species.

Ecosystems

The Sun is the source of energy for virtually all organisms and is responsible for sustaining life on the planet. The energy from the sun is harvested by trees, plants and organisms that are capable of photosynthesis. This energy is passed on to other organisms and cycled continuously.

A community of organisms that live in a certain space and interact with other living organisms as well as the environment is known as an ecosystem. These organisms are usually dependent on one another for food and survival.

Plants compete with other plants for space, water and nutrients. Animals compete for territory, shelter, food and mates. In an ecosystem, where every organism depends on another for pollination, seed dispersal and food, even the removal of one species will affect the others. This is known as 'interdependence'.

The ideal ecosystem is one in which all the species and environmental factors are in balance and the population size of the species is more or less constant.

▲ *The Sun provides energy for almost all organisms on Earth to survive*

Biotic and Abiotic Factors

Organisms in any ecosystem depend on biotic (living) and abiotic (non-living) factors.

Biotic factors affecting organisms include:

- Food (as plants or other animals)
- Microbes capable of causing diseases
- Other species that compete for the same food or space
- Predators

Abiotic factors that affect a community are:

- Light
- Temperature
- Moisture
- Soil
- Wind
- Carbon dioxide and oxygen levels

Levels of Organization

A food chain is described as a linear link of organisms starting from producers and ending in decomposers. It represents the feeding relationship within a community.

The producers are usually green plants, trees, algae or phytoplankton species capable of producing glucose from sunlight through photosynthesis. The producers are eaten by primary consumers, the herbivores. The herbivores are, in turn, eaten by the secondary consumers, the carnivores and omnivores. The secondary consumers are also known as predators and the organisms that they hunt are known as prey. Decomposers act on the dead matter of living organisms and play a crucial role as scavengers.

In a stable ecosystem, the number of prey and predators rise and fall in cycles.

▲ *A food web displays the predators and prey in an environment*

Fact File

Only about 10 percent of biomass is transferred from one trophic level to another. Respiration and excretion causes loss in biomass.

Trophic Levels

The different levels of feeding habits of organisms in a food chain are the trophic levels. They are represented by numbers, starting at level 1 which consists of the producers and then level 2 with herbivores, and further levels with predators. The apex or the topmost level is occupied by one or more carnivore species that have no predators.

Biomass pyramids are useful for representing the amount of biomass at each trophic level.

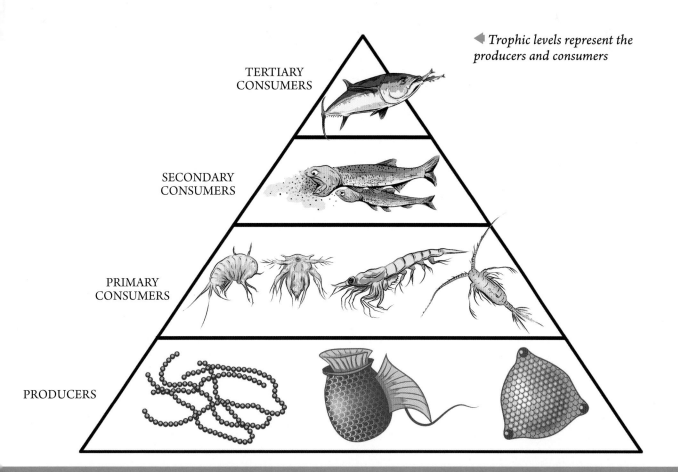

◀ *Trophic levels represent the producers and consumers*

TERTIARY CONSUMERS

SECONDARY CONSUMERS

PRIMARY CONSUMERS

PRODUCERS

Interaction with Environment

All organisms interact with their environment in complex ways. The presence of different plant, animal and microbe species contribute towards Earth's rich biodiversity. Humans play a particularly important role in damaging or conserving biodiversity and the environment.

Biodiversity

Biodiversity refers to all the different species either on the planet, or within an ecosystem. The future of humans relies on how well we conserve the biodiversity. It is also necessary to reduce or eliminate activities that harm the environment. Carbon, nitrogen, oxygen and water are important for the survival of living organisms. They are continuously cycled, ensuring a steady supply for sustaining life on the planet.

The main human activities that threaten biodiversity are:

• Global warming due to release of carbon dioxide and methane in the atmosphere

• Risk of climate change and melting of polar ice caps followed by flooding

• Destruction of habitats such as peat bogs

• Massive scale deforestation for growing need of land for houses and industries

Some useful programs that have been helpful in conserving wildlife and reducing the negative effects of growth include:

• Endangered species breeding program

• Protection of rare habitats

• Reduction in deforestation

• Decrease in carbon dioxide emission from different sources

• Recycling materials and reducing dumping of waste in landfills

• Better waste management and pollution control

Food Production and Security

Humans have been producing food for consumption through agriculture for many centuries. Food security refers to the ability to produce enough food to feed a population that is constantly growing.

Currently, a few factors that have been threatening food security include:

- Increased birth rate

- Development of new pests and disease-causing pathogens that affect plants

- Environmental variations like climate change and famines

- High cost of agricultural inputs

- Political conflicts and their effect on availability of water and food

- Changing diets of different populations

- Need for development of sustainable methods of farming and producing food

Sustainable farming and fishing can help improve efficiency of food production. This is done by reducing erosion of soil, using natural compost as much as possible, irrigation through water sources that can be replenished and other means.

Similarly, fish species in the oceans are on a decline and it is important to maintain fish stocks at a level where they can still breed normally. Introducing limits to how much fishing is allowed and controlling the size of nets is helpful in maintaining sustainable levels of fish in the oceans.

Fact File

Plastic objects can take nearly 450 years to begin decomposing and another 50 – 80 years for complete decomposition.

▲ *Food production for a growing population will be a major challenge*

▼ *Terrace farming is a type of sustainable farming that reduces soil erosion*

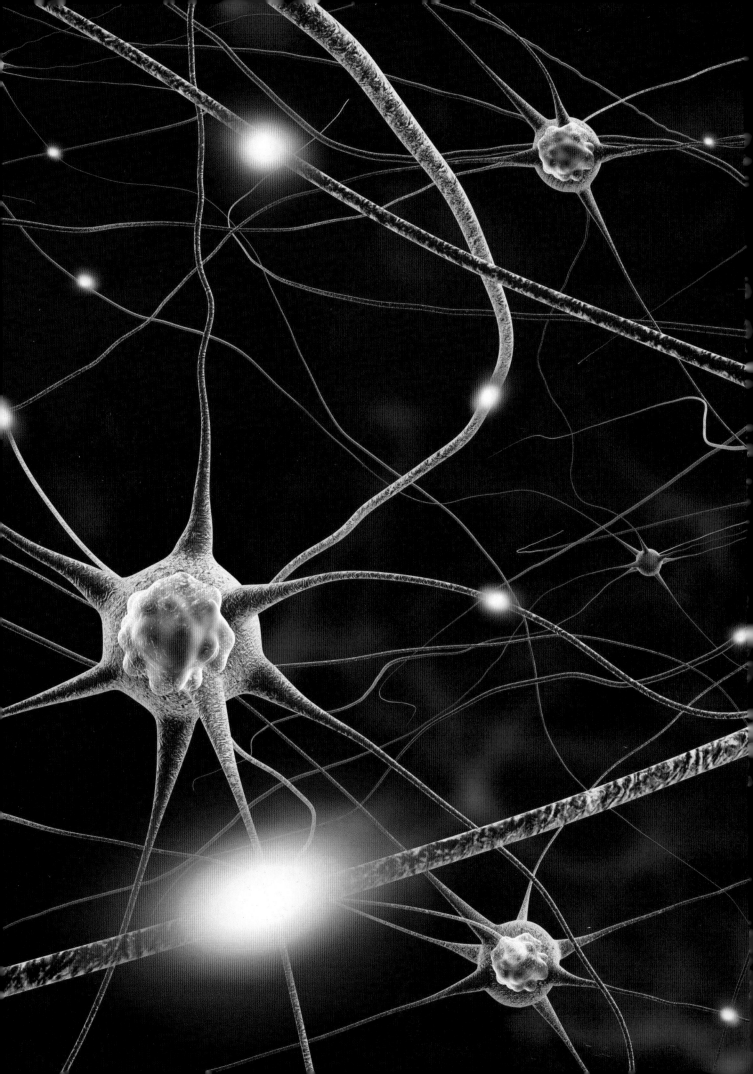